I am grateful to God for everything! And I believe that the meaning of life is to make sense of other lives. C.A., you are the meaning of my life.
Lov U

Turiano Neto

2023

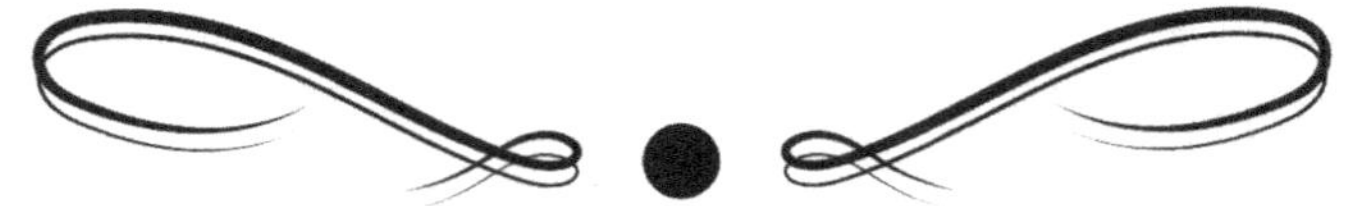

TEST COLOR PAGE

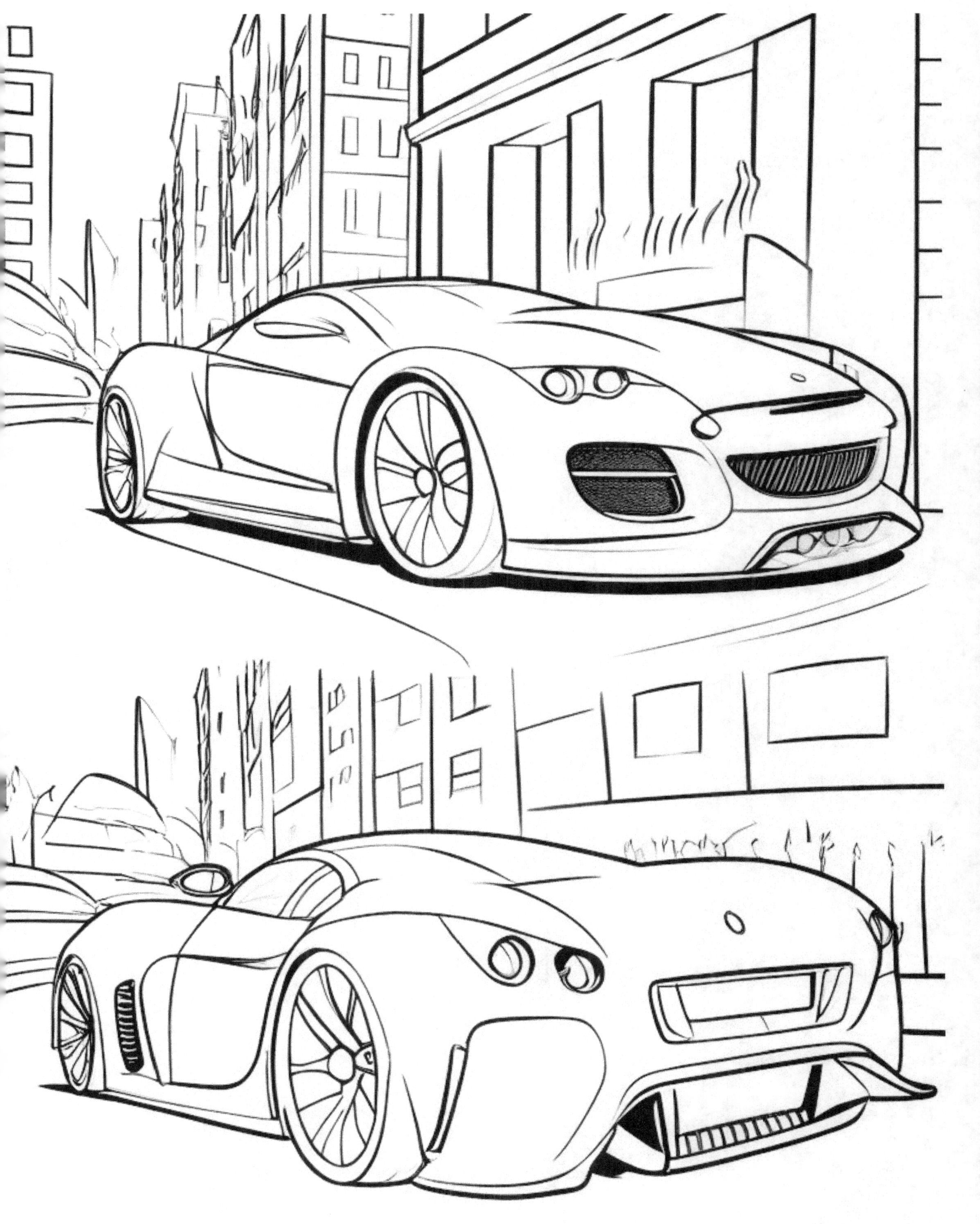

DOOD
KUVKS

www.ingramcontent.com/pod-product-compliance
Lightning Source LLC
Chambersburg PA
CBHW080940260726
48661CB00010B/4009